Peculiarities of My Perspective

Molly Dakota

Presentation by *BookLeaf Publishing*

Web: www.bookleafpub.com

E-mail: info@bookleafpub.com

ISBN: 9789360945848

First edition 2024

Dedicated to my amazing father Craig M. Ganong for always motivating me to create and love others fully. Your love of literature and people has truly inspired me. Thank you, Dad I love you!

ACKNOWLEDGEMENT

Thank you to anyone & everyone who even insinuated that my perspective was peculiar. You opened my eyes to the ordinary that is your world, which truly added color to mine. I appreciate your blank walls and judgemental hard edges because it shows the contrast that is the colorful unorganized mess of a place an artist's mind is. I believe we all have art in use we just sometimes decide to organize it into logical thoughts instead of wonderfulrific ones.

PREFACE

I hope you know that your opinions, thoughts,
and dreams matter.
DAMN IT! THEY MATTER!
So much more than you think that they do.
Stop procrastinating your self-expression, it
could save lives.

You're a wildflower
growing in a field full
of delicate neighbors
as lovely as we can be
as free as we can be
as simple as we can be
just dancing in the wind.

You! Yes, You! Pick me
if you do, please
just look for me
beneath the tall trees.

In the shade
the truth will fade
in the sun
where you laid
you could have stayed
I've never been afraid

of holding your roots down.

Little one, it's just a twirl
not the whole world
in a big ole swirl
it's just temporary.

With the season,
you will reason.
With the room,
you will bloom.

With constant change,
your petals may rearrange,
to sometimes look strange,
you're more beautiful inside and out every day.

Even if you don't believe what I say.

Baby, Find Comfort in the Corner

It's funny
the things
an extravert
hears from
the corner
of a room.

I've gone out
to bars alone
a few times
and questioned
my relevance
in these
strangers
timelines.

I used to strive
for all the love
well, ..
honestly
attention
I could get.

I didn't care

good or bad
my unfortunate
ambition.

Now I know
my add to
a strangers
conversation
is a subtraction
of their close
connection,
to take away
a comment
or voice,
an intimate
opinion.

I'm learning to
use my voice
wisely not loudly.

I want to listen
not be heard!

Alice's Mad

3

Every clock is set an hour back,
to prevent my fatal heart attack.

When you walk through your door,
tracking mud on the clean floor.

I'll be waiting by that damn phone,
wondering if you'll ever come home.

Anxious still after the thrill of you,
there's a strange book past due.

Screw the floors but I made it matter,
I miss the days you were my Mad Hatter.

Life in the Dentist's Chair

Our life is like our teeth,
Some are always straight and narrow,
Others choose to force alignments,
Spending extended time behind bars.

What you make of them,
is what you'll get.

Both are judged or idolized by strangers.
White, pure, and brilliant or
filthy, mistreated, and cracked.

Will you tend to them every day,
and make the cavities of
bad mistakes brush away?

Thinking about you on the bus ride back from Atlanta

The moments I spent with you,
I cheapened with my depression.

I've never felt things,
and never truly been happy,
I've had dreams of you being happy,
being with someone who understands,
I've thought it could be me,
and I've thought I'm not deserving.

I picture you some nights,
with a white picket fence and a dog,
I pictured myself there,
and I see myself as picket as the fence,
I don't belong,
I don't deserve to be happy.

In my deepest thoughts,
I know I don't want to be happy,
I have a fear that happy means,
I won't be funny anymore.

I think of you,
and it makes me happy,

I feel guilty as I know,
I've caused you pain,
The pain I never wanted to cause,
yet I knew I would from the start.

I'm broke,
so damn broken,
like the fence I grew up with,
I want to see you happy with,
the white picket fence and that dog.

I hope I'll be aimlessly scrolling,
a thousand thoughts from now,
and see you happy,
see you with that perfect girl,
and the white picket fence.

I know you'll be happy,
I know you'll be funny,
even when you are happy.

I think of the
whiskey-coated kisses,
we shared and I cry,
I always wanted to,
open up to you,
and I wish I did,
I can't wait to see you happy,
with a perfect girl, a dog, and a fence.

The fence that keeps out,
heartbreak and pain like me,
I will think of you for eternity.

Art of Smile Lines

8

Faces loosen,
Smiles rearrange,
Traced paths,
Never change,

Your fathers face
remains the same
in your membrane
to refrain the pain.

Parents pass
we pray ours
to be the last.

I'm a coward
to times fair hand
as more I demand.

After my rhythms
and after me
please don't sit in misery.

I love my father,
and his father too.
All shall weather

when growing
light as a feather.

As my breath passes
nothing surpasses
learn from my past
and loving your present.

Spirit Object

Most nights baby
I feel we are
a firework show
always different
flames and colors
yet somehow it's
familiarly comfortable
every time we blow up.

Other nights darling
you're those jeans
my favorite pair.

Ripped in all the
wrong seams.
Warn down
in the knees.
Tried and true
from my tripping.

Those jeans
don't fit me
the same anymore.

On some days they

just don't fit at all.
Yet, I could never
get rid of them.
This denim part of me.

Even when they
make me feel
far too small
I remember the days
when those jeans
had me standing tall.

Oh Baby Blues
I'd give anything
to have you
fit the way
you used to.

Lifeguard in the desert

This heart's been worn
this heart's been torn
tattered and abused
but wouldn't someone
still need it?

Drowning in a desert
of unrelenting dry air
heaving trying to breathe
crushing, squeezing

Will they feel the
pain so rooted in
my hard hard heart?

Immense pressure
from nothing
thousands of nothings
nothings the size of
a grain of sand
but tons of thousands
of grains
pushing down, down
on her temple.

Blood pulsing in her mind
but on the outside she's
smiling and staring at
a singular grain
laying on the table
and then she blows.

Transcribe my thoughts
into your notebooks
keep my dreams
inside your head
and fears tight
under your bed.

Will I be of use
when my eyes close
for the last time?
Will they transplant
the pain or just the organ?

Your Adolesence

Stuck in this cycle,
my heart recycled,
In your love swings,
but the true things
I'll never say to you,
I wish I would.

You have to change,
you better change,
you need to change,
you'll never change,
but that's all you'll ever need.

How can you live,
just living for yourself,
never living for much,
living you're not much,
in my world,
in this world,
you'll never be much to anyone.

Who doesn't want someone,
who really wants just anyone,
who doesn't want something,
who really wants just anything,

from you my darling.

There are people, who make me strive,
Strive to dive into every opportunity.
People who make me leap to,
Reach the steepest mountains.

Encouraging people are these,
They make me believe and make me leave,
All my fears behind,
Pull the dreams up high.
I succeed for me but also for them.

In ten years where will I be,
On top of a mountain for the world to see,
City life is always exciting,
But country life is good for writing,

My Children will be strong
like their father,
But who will he be,
When my face is worn
and torn he will love me,
And I will love him.

In the time I have to predict,
Who will I be and what will I see?

The Salty Sea Me

It's a mother fruitin'
salt sea
but at least
we're free!

Convince me
 to "be free" and
have no responsibility!

No fee doesn't mean free.
Please in this society,
guilt is free's fee.
How you owe me,
can't you see?

The man calls it poetry.
I call it a mockery!
Are you mocking me?
Looks he's been stalking me.

Laying so close that
we choke on your smoke.
I've heard too many lies to pray.
Too many lies for today.

You know I don't play.
So whatcha gonna say?
Why you being so lazy?
You'll never amaze me.

Again so soon friend

Now I'm not
complaining.

I'm truly
reframing
my position
and hope it
puts you to
ease while
these words
flow freely
from me.

Currently,
I feel

.

.

.

.

.

.

I FUCKING
hate you.

I truly

honestly
do hate
you and
all you do.

This soon
will pass
like your gas
and I'll love
you again.

My Ways Most Days

Never know it when I'm right,
my goals lost and out of sight.
Short text in the middle
of this long f*&%$in' night.

I keep walking away
from the things I like.

Eyes drenched
fist clenched
thrown wrench
on the bench.

I'm getting lost in this haze
feels like most days
I'm in a thick glaze
following this craze
disgusted in my own ways.

Most days I hesitate
most days I run late
most days I can hate
my love for myself.

Victimize the hero

in my mind
every time I get
something good
I've never understood.

Tattoo turned to
blank space
permanence
allusion
was my confusion
in the worst way.

Who are you
when all you are left
with is yourself?

Talking to your pillow
even got it dressed up
like ya
am I crazy like
duh?

I hope no one knows
baby how this blows
but straighten up and pose
you gotta post even the lows
got us on our toes
something on your nose
covered your woes.

I just need space
all at my own pace
I'm gonna retrace
back to my safe place
no more save face
but I am replaced
because I am not a disgrace.

Most days I save date
most days I relate
most days I hit plate
most days I locate
my love for myself.

Leaking Liqour

Crying so much
You offer a touch
I'm lost in my pity
You say I'm pretty
I can't see you
I can't see through
All that I do
I'm always subdued
But we'll blame it on
The stranger pawn
Who handed me a drink
Maybe next time I'll think
pour it all down the sink
Baby, I don't wanna drink!

Ink from Chicago

24

Scars are the stories
we quickly cover
with tattoos.

Their holding onto
things that aren't
even there
carrying things
they don't even need.

How will
we save them
they looked and repeated
never defeated

I've had a tan line
from a ring that rested
on my finger for years
but that's faded now
from all the sunshine
I've seen since.

Pack lightly my child
onwards and upwards.
Don't make rush

decisions when
you're bleeding.

25

Heal?

I must control
I can't unroll
the tension
deep inside
I can't lose control
I must control.

Why do we hold so close
things that often hurt us
your blisters are from
your favorite shoes
in the very front of
the closet polished
and lovingly placed.

Here the first thing on
a meticulous bookcase
your yearbook filled to
the brim with assholes
you'll never have time
in your heart for again.

Why do I hold so close
people that often hurt me
here I mumble to myself

I want to be free really
all I truly mean is alone
I waste hours pleasing
the unpleasant.

Will we hold close
That which heals us?

We forget to
sing and dance
we must try
hopes high.

Change in your own way
play in the slow lane
travel at your own speed
take care of your needs.

Wave

Cheerful new eyes open
Where storm clouds suspend
To the new world pretend
All your emotions have mend
When you return home
To comprehend
All our stories
Laid down in pen

Mornings promising embrace
Lifts me out of bed
Like a fresh new
Wave ever free
Moving on momentum
And natural spiritual force
Not hesitant or wery
That the ever so
Certainty of crashing
Down onto the shore
Is moments away
But still moving
Freely without
Delay as if
To one day move
and everyday

metaphorically a piece
and another move past
This shore into the land
Up the trees
Into the sky
And then falling gently
back into the ocean to try again.

Dried Flowers

The love was lacking in your letter
but traces linger where it was drug
across the page to somewhere else.

Where did you pull it if it
no longer belongs here?

Dried flowers hang soon to be pressed
then eventually filed safely away.

Those fresh memories of our youth
now brittle and dried out by the clock
some damaged in the frigid climate
that world outside of ours.

What will I be remembered for?

Some things can't live forever.
Magic is a moment almost as
disposable as you and I.

All we need is hope and great
expectations my flickering love.

Queens of Our Hearts

31

They don't care
who they are dear.
So, don't you dare!
They're pretty here
and that's enough.

They asked where
I was headed
the answer
they dreaded.

Liars beheaded
the Queens
of our hearts.

Please don't digress!
I detest
to just be
some dress
you slipt off
last night.

Yeah, I'll put up a fight!

Cement Children

Looking up to you
Open minded little one he
never knew what you would do
closed eyes will never see
what everyone can really be
your little son never asked for life
it was always your choice
yet you still hold your strife
you ripped away his voice
knotted his throat
stapled his lips closed
you must have broken
mirrors the luck is gone
hidden away behind the years
when will it dawn upon
you and your child's ears
this is your imprint
like cement you pushed
your hand down
covered the mouth
and shushed
these depressing frowns
where once innocent smiles
you're broken promises and closed doors
are building up a dam

his waters never flowing anymore
he used to be so brave now a lamb
quiet praying for a break
why do you always have to take take take
we have nothing more to give.

You too?

What did they do?
I can't even see you.
Through what they
did to you.

You don't have to do,
Oh, you don't have to.
I have had to and hadn't.
I'm sadden to and mad too.
Sure sounds like you had to.
Ya sounds like they had you.

Where is past you?
Now rep'n their tattoo
and you don't know you
what to do wondering why
I'm coming at you.

You know you can't
hold me back too.

I am (written in 2012 and happy to finally be with you)

I am ambitious and artistic,
I wonder how the world is so cruel,
I hear the bigamists rule,
I see people stop being realistic,
I want some chivalry,
I am ambitious and artistic.

I pretend there is nothing wrong,
I feel my feelings through song,
I touch the world with curiosity,
I worry for the future unknown,
I cry to see innocence die,
I am ambitious and artistic.

I understand nothing's endless,
I say my words are relentless,
I dream of lives and minds coexisting,
I try to make an imprint of my existence,
I am ambitious and artistic.

"I was never really good with words anyway"

No ink,
No thoughts,
No time,

This lousy pen
can only get
out every other letter.

These precious words
just won't come out.
Damned cuz it's
the same with my mouth.

My words are fading out.
Back to screaming
scribbles in my mind.

I write,
I expect
my words
to move me
enough to
share them
with anyone else.

Yet I can't even
convince me
it's good enough
to even be done at all.

Laying here
half songs,
half books,
starts to ideas,
film treatments,
and illegible words
of no use to anyone.

I guess that's
what all of this is
if I don't finish it.

So many hours
of my heartache
and life wasted.

Pleading with myself
for just the right
words to write down.

That's all I think
about sometimes
just the right

word to write down.

Honestly,
not even just
to write down.

Getting the right
words out of my
mouth in an
appropriate
response time
is rare to be kind.

I never know the words
at all
I suppose...

I hope the words of this book
brought you peace & please
remember I love you truly.
This will never feel done
but I needed to get it out.
I wish you do the same because I really need
your art my friend.

You don't believe me but I do.
We understand each other.

.

.

.

I love you and your ideas.